WITHDRAWN

D0503286

Published by
Black Dog & Leventhal Publishers, Inc.
151 West 19th Street
New York, NY 10011

Distributed by
Workman Publishing Company
708 Broadway
New York, NY 10003

Cover and interior design by 27.12 Design, Ltd.

Manufactured in China

ISBN: 1-57912-168-3

h g f e d c b

Library of Congress Cataloging-in-Publication Data available upon request

MINNESOTA

BY ERIK BRUUN

illustrated by

RICK PETERSON

BLACK DOG
& LEVENTHAL
PUBLISHERS
NEW YORK

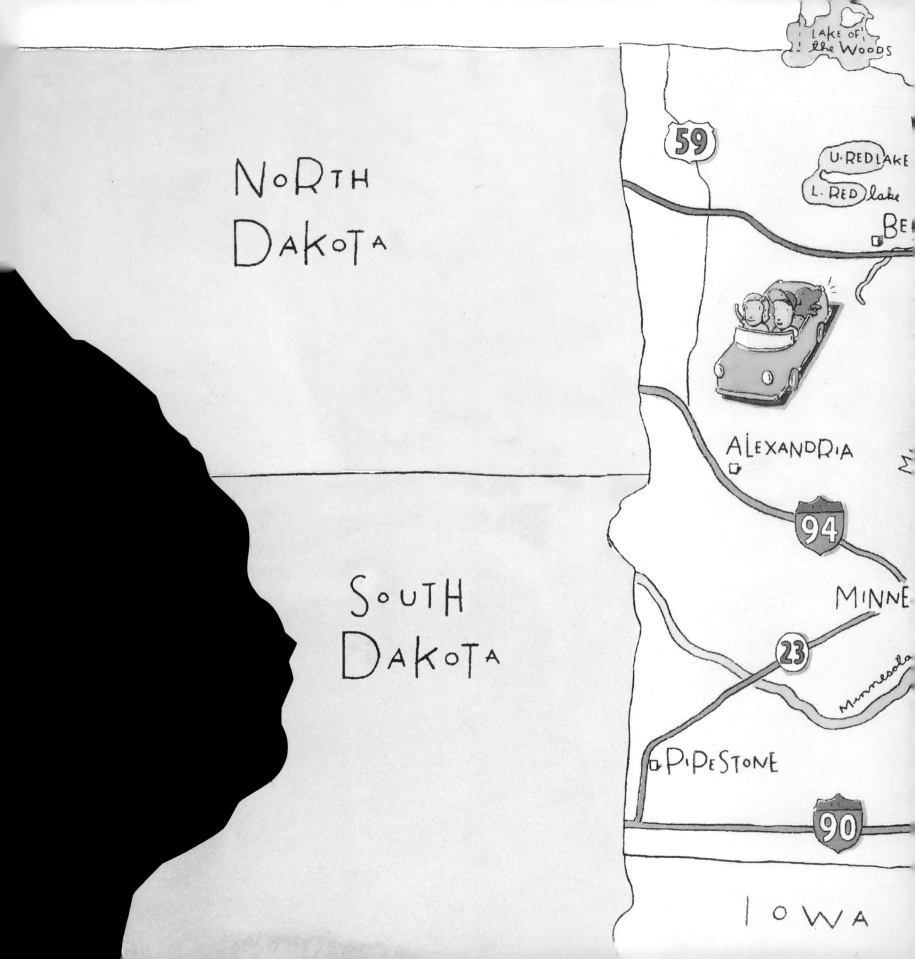

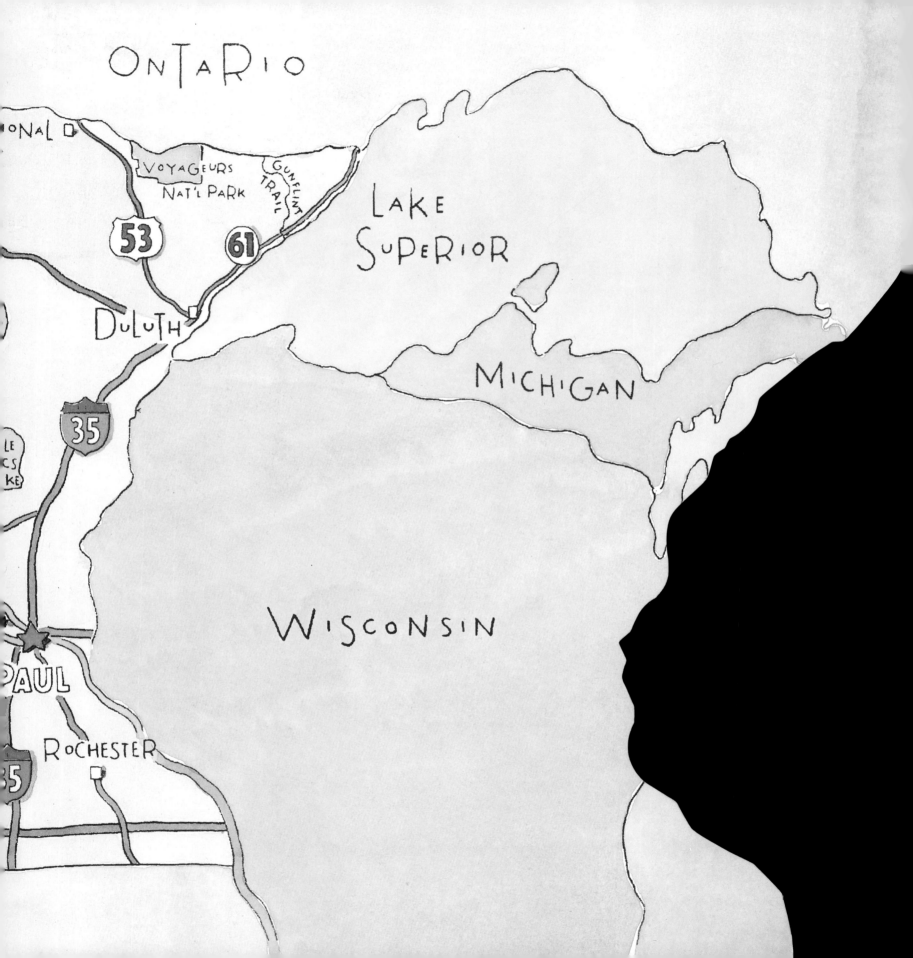

PAUL BUNYAN AND
HIS BLUE OX, BABE

Welcome to Minnesota! My name is Scott Andersen. My friend Elsa Wilson is visiting me so I'm going to show her lots of fun things about Minnesota. People call it the land of sky-blue waters, and the waters really are pretty neat. It's something to see. But we're not just going to see lakes and waterfalls, we're also going to look up at giant statues of Paul Bunyan and his blue ox, Babe, cross the wide open prairie that my ancestors settled, and shop at the world's largest indoor shopping mall.

Wow, Scott, Minnesota sounds like a cool state. This is my dog Pumpkin— he wants to learn about Minnesota. So, Scott, where do we start?

Q. What sport was Minnesota Governor Jesse Ventura famous for before he was elected?

Where the first explorers arrived—Duluth. Then we'll check out the beautiful northern country, circle on down through the vast Plains, come up the winding Mississippi River, and end our journey in the busy Twin Cities of Minneapolis and St. Paul, our state capital. That'll cover everything from the biggest fresh water lake in the world to the world's largest open pit-iron mine to the famous sled dog marathon to the town where the infamous outlaw Jesse James tried to rob a bank.

I can't wait—let's go!

GOVERNOR AND FORMER PRO-WRESTLER JESSE VENTURA

A. Teeth-gnashing, muscle-grinding professional wrestling.

DULUTH WAS
BUILT ON A HILL

So this is Duluth?

Not too bad, is it? It used to be one of the hustlingest, bustlingest cities in the United States. It was one of the fastest growing cities in America after it became a major hub of the Northern Pacific Railroad, the first railroad to cross the country. Carved out of a steep hillside on the shore of Lake Superior, Duluth was a booming port and manufacturing city. By the late 1800s there were 85 millionaires in the city (and being a millionaire back then meant you were really, really rich), more than any other U. S. city of a similar population.

Wow! But how did all those people start out here in the first place?

Duluth is named after Daniel Greysolon, Sieur Du Luth, one of the first European fur trappers to visit Minnesota.

DANIEL GREYSOLON, SIEUR DULUTH

Q. Why did Duluth dub itself "the air-conditioned city" in the early 1900s?

He crossed the huge Lake Superior in 1679 in a canoe! He set up camp here and claimed the land for France. A lot of other trappers, called "voyageurs" (French for "travelers"), followed him and made Duluth a big fur trading center.

Were they the first people here?

No. Actually, Native American Indians came to this area more than 10,000 years ago. They hunted animals as big as elephants called mastodons and mammoths. When Du Luth landed here there were two main tribes. The Dakota, also known as the Sioux, were in the woods in eastern and northern Minnesota. They lived in homes made of bark called wigwams and tents made from animal skins. Starting in the 1600s another tribe moved into Minnesota from the east called the Ojibway, or Chippewa. Eventually the Chippewa, who had gotten guns from European settlers, forced the Sioux west out into the Great Plains.

the AIR-CONDITIONED CITY

A. To attract too-hot tourists from the South.

What about all this water?
Is that the ocean? Look at the waves!

Although it's so big and wavy it looks like the ocean, that's actually Lake Superior, the very lake that the first explorer crossed. It's the largest freshwater lake in the world and is up to a quarter-mile deep, more than 400 miles long and 160 miles wide, almost as big as the state of Minnesota itself. In fact, if you took all the water in Lake Superior and dumped it over North America, the continent would be swimming under three feet of water. And if you tried to fit all the other great lakes into Lake Superior, you'd still have room for three more lakes the size of Lake Erie. It's so big that it acts like an ocean and awesome storms have swept across creating giant waves that have sunk many boats.

IRON ORE BOAT

Hey, check out that ship—it's huge! It doesn't look like it could sink.

Q. What is the third largest statue in the United States?

That's an iron ore boat. Ships as long as 1,000 feet (almost one fifth of a mile long!) come to Duluth to take away as much iron ore and coal as you can fit in 600 rail cars. They use an incredible engineering contraption called the Aerial Lift Bridge, which has a large steel deck that lifts boats into a narrow canal that connects to Lake Superior.

So they don't just trade fur anymore.

No, Minnesota has eased up on our furry friends. Now its biggest exports are coal, iron ore, and wheat, which are all shipped out of Duluth. More than a hundred years ago they discovered huge deposits of iron. Minnesota has been the top iron-mining state in the nation since 1901. Duluth used to be a booming port and steel town, which is what made it so wealthy. Unfortunately, although the mills that converted the iron to steel created lots of jobs, they also led to pollution in Lake Superior. The state and companies have done a lot of work to start to repair the environmental damage.

WE FOUND IT!

YEP! YEP? YEP!

IRON WAS DISCOVERED IN MINNESOTA MORE THAN 100 YEARS AGO

A. The 81-foot-tall Iron Man at Ironworld in Chisholm. Only the Statue of Liberty and St. Louis Arch are larger.

THE MESABI RANGE

So, Minnesota's
the top iron-mining state?
Where does the iron come from?

Just west of here in an area called the Iron Range. Starting in the 1880s, prospectors discovered a series of iron "veins." One of them, the Mesabi Range, was 120 miles long and full of the metal. Seven brothers named Merritt found the iron ore there. It produced up to a third of the world's iron supply until the 1950s! Thousands of immigrants from central and southern Europe poured into Minnesota to work in the giant open-pit mines and the factories that turned the iron into steel. Minnesota's steel and iron helped build the country and arm the nation during World Wars I and II. Minnesota's mines shaped American history.

Wow! Can you still see the mines today?

Q. Lots of iron was discovered in the Cuyuna Range—how did the range get its name?

You sure can. The Hull-Rust-Mahoning Mine in Hibbing is the world's largest open-pit iron mine. It's three miles long and 500 feet deep (more than one and a half football fields straight down!). It still operates every once in a while when the other mines around the country aren't producing enough iron to supply builders. Giant shovels as big as buildings dump their loads onto 200-ton trucks (which equals 400,000 pounds, the weight of almost 4,000 of your friends). The tires on the trucks are 10 feet high. You can learn everything you ever wanted to know about mining in Chisholm at the Ironworld Discovery Center and the Minnesota Museum of Mining.

What a wacky museum. Are there other cool museums to see nearby?

Yes. You can visit the United States Hockey Hall of Fame in nearby Eveleth. Hockey is a big sport in the chilly state of Minnesota.

 The range was named by Cuyler Adams, who discovered the iron deposit in 1911, and combined the first three letters of his name with the name of his dog, Una.

Brrrr. It's cold... and windy.

Get ready to bundle up. This part of Minnesota—well, really all of Minnesota—gets positively polar in the winter. The water in Lake Superior barely ekes above 40 degrees (just eight degrees over freezing) in the summer, and it sometimes freezes over during the winter. Inland, the air temperature can fall to 50 or even 60 degrees below zero! When it gets that cold, strange things happen. Airplanes sound louder. Eyebrows freeze. And be careful not to stick your tongue on a lamppost, because you won't get it back.

Minnesotans are ready for it, though. In the cities, they put stores on the second floors of buildings and everybody uses overpasses to cross the streets. In Minneapolis, you can walk from one end of the city to the other without touching the sidewalk! Sometimes when we have parades, the only people on the street are the marchers. Everyone else is lined up along windows inside.

Weird. I have to say, winter doesn't sound very fun.

Q. Can you guess what winter vehicle was built in Roseau, Minnesota, in 1953?

You just have to learn how to enjoy yourself Minnesota style. We do lots of cool things when it's cold outside. Ice skating. Ice fishing. Skiing. Snow jumping. Hockey. Broomball. Snow sculpting. There's even a famous race called the John Beargrease Sled Dog Marathon that starts right here in Duluth. It's a 500-mile race in honor of a rugged Ojibwe Indian who delivered mail up and down Lake Superior's North Shore from 1887 to 1900. It's a very exciting start with lots of leaping dogs and shouting spectators.

ICE FISHING ON THE LAKE

I don't think Pumpkin has 500 miles of running in her...

The winner gets $10,000.

JOHN BEARGREASE
SLED DOG MARATHON

When does she start?

 A. The slippery-slope defying snowmobile.

Don't worry Pumpkin, we won't make you pull us in a sled up the North Shore. The North Shore is one of the most spectacular patches of soaring cliffs, tumbling waterfalls, and cobblestone beaches in the nation. Think wild beauty.

I don't need to think it, I see it!
How'd it get like this?

The glaciers helped create this rugged coast 10,000 years ago, carving gorges into the hillsides and creating scenic and deep rivers. There are seven state parks along the 80-mile coast between Duluth and the Canadian border. You can travel the North Shore by car on Route 61 or go by foot on the Superior Hiking Trail. Some people call it one of the best trails in the world, and it has beautiful campgrounds along the way.

PORTAGING IN the BOUNDARY WATERS

Q. What is Minnesota's state grain?

Most of the region is preserved as part of the Superior National Forest. The northern section is 15,000 square miles and is known as the Boundary Waters Canoe Area Wilderness. It is the country's first wilderness area set aside for canoeing. You can paddle from one stunning lake to the next. On the northern tip is Grand Portage, once one of the busiest fur trading posts on the Great Lakes. The Grand Portage National Monument has a reconstructed stockade that is terrific fun. Just like the trading post days 200 years ago, the stockade has Native American tipis and wigwams, canoes as long as 36 feet, and reenactments of the old life with people firing muskets and making birch canoes. The whole region is a natural paradise.

Speaking of nature, what was that howling noise?

Wolves. There are more than 2,000 wolves in northeastern Minnesota, the largest number east of the Rocky Mountains. They may seem scary, but wolves are very important animals in keeping the natural ecosystem in balance. Wolves prevent overgrazing of forests by preying on animals such as deer and rabbits that eat the low vegetation.

All this talk of wolves is scaring Pumpkin.

A. Wild rice. It grows in marshes in northern Minnesota.

What, more lakes?

Yep. This is the Lake of the Woods, on the northern tip of Minnesota. It's one of Minnesota's many beautiful lakes.

Is that why some people call Minnesota the "Land of 10,000 Lakes"?

"MINNESOTA" COMES FROM A DAKOTA INDIAN WORD MEANING "CLOUD REFLECTING WATER"

Uh-huh, even though there are really more like 15,000 lakes! We have lakes everywhere, especially in the north. The name "Minnesota" comes from a Dakota Indian word meaning "cloud-reflecting water." We Minnesotans know how to enjoy our lakes. There are 2 million boats in Minnesota, nearly one for every two people in the state. Half the people fish, and we love to eat what we catch—walleye, whitefish, and, of course, lake trout are all favorites. I bet you didn't know Minnesota introduced water skiing to the world. In 1922, at Lake Pepin, a young man strapped on a pair of skis, attached himself to a boat, and away he went—the new sport of water skiing had been invented.

Q. What kind of fish in the Minnesota lakes is so big it sometimes eats ducks?

The Lake of the Woods is one of the largest lakes. We share it with Canada. In fact, this part of Minnesota at the Northwest Angle is the most northern point in the Lower 48 states. That's why some people call Minnesota the "North Star State."

Northwest Angle is a very odd place. Even though it's part of Minnesota, you can't get to it by road from the United States without going through Canada. The problem dates back to a border dispute between England and America nearly 200 years ago. It is mainly state forest with some fishing areas and small resorts. Some of the people who live here want to secede from the United States and join Canada because they are basically in Canada already.

GO TO CANADA, TAKE A RIGHT AT the U.S., THEN GO RIGHT TOWARD CANADA

NOW LEAVING CANADA

NORTHWEST ANGLE

CANADA

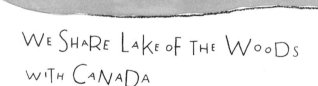
WE SHARE LAKE OF THE WOODS WITH CANADA

 A. Muskellunges (also called "Muskies") are enormous pikes that can weigh as much as 80 pounds and measure as long as 6 feet.

So, there was an argument between the British and the Americans? But I thought French trappers settled Minnesota. When did the British and Americans get here?

Good question. The answer is kind of complicated. The French had trading posts along Minnesota's lakes and rivers until 1763, when England defeated France in the French and Indian War and took control of Canada and part of Minnesota. When we won the American Revolution twenty years later, we got England's part of Minnesota. In 1803, President Thomas Jefferson bought France's piece that was west of the Mississippi River, so all of Minnesota belonged to the United States.

The first U.S. soldiers arrived here in 1819 and began building Fort Snelling on the Mississippi River. Two years later the first American settlers came to farm and cut lumber. Minnesota became the nation's 32nd state on May 11, 1858.

What did the Indians think about that?

Q. Minnesota was the first Northern state to contribute what to the Civil War?

They weren't too happy. In fact, there was a big war. The Dakota sold their land to the United States in the 1850s. As part of the deal, the government was supposed to give them supplies and food. But when the Civil War erupted in 1861, the government stopped providing food, so in order to survive the Indians started hunting again on the settlers' land. That didn't please the settlers very much, and fighting broke out.

Because many of Minnesota's young men had left to fight in the Civil War, the Indians were very successful at first. Towns were burned to the ground and nearly 500 settlers were killed. Eventually, though, a special army was raised to defeat and capture the Indians, and 38 Dakota were hanged. Many people think that the Indians were treated unfairly.

FORT SNELLING

YA, SURE, WE'LL GO.

 A. Men. Minnesota was the first Northern state to offer volunteer soldiers to the cause.

That sounds awful.

I know, it's not such a fun story. Let's go to Grand Rapids for something cheerier, the birthplace of Judy Garland.

As in Dorothy singing "Somewhere Over the Rainbow" in *The Wizard of Oz*? Cool-e-o.

JUDY GARLAND WAS FROM MINNESOTA

That's the one! Judy Garland's original name was Frances Gumm— you can see why it was changed for the movies—and she only lived in Grand Rapids for her first four years. But Grand Rapids has made the most of it. There is an annual Judy Garland Festival—with Munchkins and all. Even though we missed the festival, we can visit the Judy Garland Birthplace—her home in Grand Rapids—and the Children's Discovery Museum, which has a silver Winkie sword from the Wicked Witch of the West's fortress and a colorful coat from Emerald City. There is even an exhibit about Judy Garland at Old Central School, which she attended as a toddler.

Q. What famous Minnesotan changed his name to a symbol?

Look! There's a yellow-brick path at the school. Are there any other famous people from Minnesota?

GOOD GRIEF!

Lots. Charles Schulz, who did the Peanuts cartoon and created Snoopy, came from Minneapolis. The famous folk singer Bob Dylan who wrote "Blowin' in the Wind" and "The Times Are A-Changin'" was born in Duluth as Robert Zimmerman. Two of America's most famous writers came from Minnesota: Sinclair Lewis, who was the first American to win the Nobel Prize for literature, grew up in a small Minnesota town and wrote about it in his book *Main Street*. F. Scott Fitzgerald, who wrote *The Great Gatsby*, came from St. Paul.

CHARLES SCHULZ CREATED SNOOPY AND THE PEANUTS CARTOON

BOB DYLAN

PRINCE?

 A. The rock star Prince, born as Prince Rogers Nelson, changed his name to a symbol from 1993 to 2000. Prince is originally from Minneapolis.

Hey, Who's this guy Paul Bunyan? Everywhere I turn I see his name. Paul Bunyan restaurants. Paul Bunyan bike trails. Paul Bunyan motels. Who the heck was Paul Bunyan?

PAUL BUNYAN
BIKE TRAIL

Paul Bunyan was more than a person. He was a legend— a great lumberjack who could fell giant trees with a single swipe of his axe. The first stories about Paul Bunyan and his giant blue ox, Babe, appeared in the early 1900s. And, just like Bunyan, some of the tales are pretty tall. One story has him scooping out the Great Lakes to make bowls of water for Babe to drink from. Paul Bunyan is part of the mythology of logging in Minnesota, and logging has been a huge part of this state's history.

"MINNESOTA'S LAKES were FORMED WHEN PAUL BUNYAN'S FOOTSTEPS FILLED WITH WATER"

Well, the statues are neat and big!

Q. According to legend, who was Paul Bunyan's sweetheart?

The first one was an 18-footer in Bemidji built in 1937 by the local Rotary Club. That started it all. The biggest one is 33 feet high outside of the Paul Bunyan History Museum in Akeley. There's a 100-mile Paul Bunyan State Trail with a 26-foot monument on one end and an entire Paul Bunyan Amusement Center on the other.

When it comes to building statues, we Minnesotans just can't stop. There are giant mascots all over the state. The town of Black Duck has a 16-foot wooden black duck. Fergus Falls in Otter Tail County has a 22-foot concrete otter that sits at the edge of a lake. Rothsay has a 13-by-18-foot concrete prairie chicken. Downtown Pelican Rapids boasts a 15-foot—you guessed it—pelican. Minnesota also claims a 25-foot-long serpent named Kanabec in Serpent Lake, a 20-foot fiberglass loon floating on Silver Lake, and a 26-foot Smokey the Bear statue in International Falls.

A couple of the sculptures refer back to some of our Scandanavian ancestors. In Menahga there is a 12-foot statue of a Finnish saint—St. Urho, who warded off a plague of grasshoppers—holding a pitchfork with a grasshopper on one of the tines. Finally, in Alexandria, there is Big Ole, who's 26 feet tall and wears a Viking skirt, spear, and shield.

A. Lucetta Diana Kensack. You can find a 17-foot statue of her in Hackensack, Minnesota.

Speaking of Scandanavians, didn't you say your ancestors came over from up north?

Yep, my family's from Norway. My great-great-grandfather arrived here in the 1870s to build a farm, make a fresh start in life. Many Norwegians, Swedes, and others from northern Europe came to this part of the United States. They were used to the weather, I guess. Life started out rough on the edge of the Great Prairie, but they built Minnesota into a great state.

MANY NORTHERN EUROPEANS MOVED TO MINNESOTA IN THE EARLY DAYS

What prairie?

The great rolling plains that run from here west to the Rocky Mountains. When my ancestors first arrived, it was a sea of wild grassland broken up by wet prairie, sedge meadows, and the occasional geological oddity, like red cliffs made of sparkly rocks called quartz. Thousands of years ago glaciers carried soil from Canada south into this area. When the great ice sheets melted, soil that was as much as 400 feet

Q. Why do crowds of children gather in a parking lot every summer Wednesday afternoon in Nisswa?

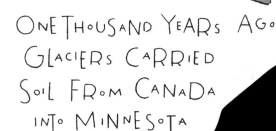

thick seeped onto the midlands of the United States, including southern and western Minnesota. When the settlers came they cut through the soil in order to start farms. The sod was so thick, many settlers built their first homes from bricks made out of it. These buildings were called sod houses. We don't see the prairies today because this soil was so fertile that almost all of the original prairies in Minnesota have been turned into cropland.

ONE THOUSAND YEARS AGO GLACIERS CARRIED SOIL FROM CANADA INTO MINNESOTA

Don't gophers live in the prairie?

Yep. That's how Minnesota got the nickname "The Gopher State." In 1859 there was a cartoon that made fun of the Minnesotans who wanted a railroad built through the prairie by depicting them as gophers wearing top hats.

MINNESOTA IS NICKNAMED "THE GOPHER STATE"

A. To place turtles in the town's weekly turtle races. The grand prize is $5.

29

When the railroad was built, Minnesotans could transport their lumber and grain to other parts of the country. Lumber from Minnesota was used to help build houses, bridges, and ships for the rapidly growing towns and cities across the United States. Loggers felled entire forests, especially in eastern and northern Minnesota.

What about the farmers?

They planted wheat fields that covered all of western Minnesota. Minnesota farms grew more wheat than any other state. Mills ground the wheat into flour, which was used for bread. This, combined with the raising of dairy cattle in eastern Minnesota to make butter

Q. What is the state drink of Minnesota?

and milk, led some people to call Minnesota the "Bread and Butter State."

Are there still a lot of farmers?

Tens of thousands of them. We raise 5 million hogs and 40 million turkeys a year. Dairy cows, eggs, milk, turkeys, wheat, oats, soybeans, barley, corn, hay, potatoes, and beef cattle—you name it, and we grow it. In fact, Minnesota grows more sugar beets than any other state in the nation. You'll see

when we get to Minneapolis the headquarters of Cargill, the largest privately owned company in the United States. The company distributes farm products. Minnesota farms haven't just produced amber waves of grain. They've also helped build our towering cities.

A. Moo juice, better known as milk.

31

Time to visit some sights in southern Minnesota. Want to see where the original little house on the prairie was?

You mean from the TV show
Little House on the Prairie
That sounds like fun.

Laura Ingalls Wilder, who wrote eight books that inspired the famous television show, lived in a house made of mud with a single greased-paper window in Walnut Grove when she was a little girl. It was the setting for her first book, *Little House in the Big Woods*. Her family suffered from grasshopper plagues, scarlet fever, and starvation. Most of the house was wiped out in a flood, but there is a museum about Wilder and life on the prairie.

It sounds like prairie living was kind of tough.
So, where to next?

Q. True or false, Minnesotans live longer than people from any other state?

New Ulm is pretty neat. It was settled by Germans in the 1860s. They have a 32-foot sculpture of a German warrior named Hermann, who defeated a large Roman army that invaded his country 2,000 years ago. The statue stands on top of a 70-foot dome.

Plagues, starvation, warriors— can we talk about something a bit nicer?

How about the Pipestone National Monument? It's a beautiful, sacred place. Emerging out of the plains, the hard red rock cliffs of Sioux quartzite were formed more than a billion years ago. Some Indian tribes believe this was where the Great Spirit created people. Thin, red, hard clay covers the quartz. Indians have made peace pipes and other objects out of the clay for centuries.

THE PIPESTONE NATIONAL MONUMENT

A. Almost true. The average Minnesotan lives 76 years. Only Hawaiians live longer.

IN 1876
JESSE JAMES AND
HIS GANG INVADED
NORTHFIELD

Next stop, Northfield—"The Little Town That Defeated the Jesse James Gang."

Wow—that sounds like a big deal. But who was Jesse James?

He was the most notorious bank robber of the Old West. In 1876, Jesse and his brother Frank, the three Younger brothers (Jim, Bob, and Cole), and the rest of the James-Younger gang ambled into Northfield armed to the teeth to rob Northfield's First National Bank. But as they were getting ready to make the heist, a local man realized what they were up to and shouted, "Get your guns, boys, they're robbing the bank!" A big shootout erupted. A lot of Civil War veterans happened to live in Northfield, and they helped gun down most of the gang members. Still, Jesse and Frank James escaped. Every year, the weekend after Labor Day, the residents of Northfield dress up and reenact the historic bank raid.

Minnesotans are tougher than they look! It seems so peaceful now.

Q. What famous Minnesotan was called "Lucky Lindy"?

It's funny, because Northfield's motto is "Home of Cows, Colleges, and Contentment." St. Olaf is a Lutheran college in Northfield that was founded by Norwegian immigrants. Its choirs and orchestras have an international reputation. And Carleton College is one of the best small colleges in the country. The local radio station, WCAL, was the first listener-supported radio station in the country. Plus, there was a famous economist from Northfield named Thorstein Veblein who made up the term "conspicuous consumption," which is when people do a lot of shopping to show off.

"NORTHFIELD: HOME OF COWS, COLLEGES AND CONTENTMENT"

People here sound smart.

Smart, yes, but sometimes they're not so good with languages. Cannon River got its name from the French term La Riviere aux can-ots, which means "the river of canoes." English-speaking settlers pronounced the word "canots" the same way, but changed its meaning from "canoes" to "cannons." Oops.

WHERE'S FRANCE?

 Charles Lindbergh of Little Falls. In 1927, he became the first person to fly an airplane across the Atlantic Ocean by himself. Talk about luck!

35

MAYO CLINIC 1889

Bank heists and brainiacs—now what?

Let's check out Rochester, a small city with a big reputation. More than 300,000 people come to Rochester every year to visit the Mayo Clinic, the world's first, largest, and most famous private medical facility. William Worrall Mayo started the clinic n 1889. His sons, William and Charles, also became doctors, and then their sons became doctors, too. They all helped establish the clinic as one of the finest in the world.

I've noticed that a lot of people from Minnesota do good things.

That's true. Some of the most important progressive American judges and politicians from the second half of the 1900s came from Minnesota. William O. Douglas served on the Supreme Court longer than any other person. From 1939 to 1975, he was one of the most influential voices to protect the rights of individual Americans. Supreme Court Justices Warren

Q. What Minnesotan won the Nobel Peace Prize for overseeing a treaty that made war illegal?

Burger and Harry Blackmun grew up together in St. Paul. They even played tennis with each other as boys.

Three liberal Democrats from Minnesota all ran for President. Hubert Humphrey, who was called "The Happy Warrior" for his passionate support of liberal causes like the rights of blacks, was Vice President under Lyndon Johnson and ran for President against Richard Nixon in 1968. Minnesota Senator Eugene McCarthy also ran for President that year. Another senator, Walter Mondale, was Vice President under President Jimmy Carter in the 1970s. He ran for President in 1984 against Ronald Reagan. Unfortunately, all of these Gopher-staters lost their elections.

And Minnesotans like to vote, too. Four out of every five Minnesota adults is a registered voter, more than any other state except North Dakota.

HUBERT HUMPHREY

FOUR OUT OF FIVE MINNESOTANS IS A REGISTERED VOTER

 A. Frank C. Kellogg, a driving force behind the Kellogg-Briand Peace Pact of 1928.

DOWNTOWN
LANESBORO

This town is beautiful!

We're in Lanesboro. The National Trust for Historical Preservation—a cool organization that preserves historic buildings, neighborhoods, and other landmarks—gave Lanesboro the Great American Main Street award for its vibrant downtown. It all started when they built a bicycle trail through town in the 1980s. All of a sudden, people started coming to Lanesboro. A downtown movie theater opened, artists launched a gallery, a cultural center was built. Interest just kept growing until Lanesboro became a hive of activity. In fact, more bicycle trails were built all over southeastern Minnesota. Minnesota has the second most bicycle trails in the country, and they are adding more all the time.

That's great. You can see a lot more from a bicycle than a car.

38

Q. What Minnesota Supreme Court judge used to be a "Purple People Eater," the nickname for players on Minnesota's football team?

Yeah, it'd be hard to drive down a path in the woods with a car! But a horse and buggy would work for that, like the Amish ones down the road in Harmony. Families of the Old Order Amish from Ohio started moving to Harmony in 1974. The Amish are a very traditional group that speaks an old German dialect and lives by strict rules derived from the Bible. Their main belief is the rejection of material goods, so they don't use the modern things—like cars, computers, or even sneakers—that we do. When the Amish arrived in Harmony they bought farmhouses, tore out the electricity and plumbing, and built windmills. They cover their hair, wear dark clothes, and refuse to be photographed. But although the Amish live by stern rules, they are often very friendly people.

THE AMISH USE BUGGIES INSTEAD OF CARS.

They don't use electricity or wear sneakers?!
I guess they won't be going with us
to the Mall of America.

You've got that right—I don't think the Amish are shopaholic types. Before we head to the mall, though, let's make a quick trip up the Mississippi River.

 The Honorable Alan Page, who was a Minnesota Vikings football defensive tackle.

THE MISSISSIPPI RIVER,
THE LONGEST RIVER IN THE U.S.,
STARTS IN MINNESOTA

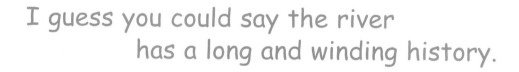

The Mississippi River starts in Lake Itasca in northern Minnesota, winds its way through Minneapolis and St. Paul, and then serves as the border with Wisconsin. After leaving Minnesota, the mighty river meanders through the center of the country and empties into the Gulf of Mexico. It is the longest river in the United States and the third largest river system in the world. Known as Old Man River, it served as the main entryway for settlers and commerce in Minnesota's early history. Historic towns line the waterway. Bike trails run alongside the riverbanks and several museums chart the region's history, including one in a restored paddlewheel boat.

I guess you could say the river
          has a long and winding history.

Ugh. But it's true. And many people say the section of the river from below Minneapolis to the Iowa border is the most attractive. With bluffs up to 575-feet high in Winona, there are incredible views. It's also a birdwatcher's

Q. What is the state bird of Minnesota?
(Hint: it's kind of "crazy.")

paradise. Birds migrate up and down the river. You can see pelicans and warblers in the spring. There is an Eagle Watch Observatory in Wabasha where you can watch bald eagles during the winter.

That is pretty cool. You know, nature's nice and all, but I want to see the Mall of America.

Okay, okay. South of the Twin Cities in Bloomington, this megalithic mall is the largest of its kind in the nation and the Number One attraction in Minnesota. Opened in 1992, it has 520 stores, but that's the least of it. There is a 1.2 million-gallon aquarium, a pirate-ship playground, a virtual submarine ride, a bowling alley, a seven-acre theme park—complete with rollercoaster—and a 75-seat Chapel of Love where they perform an average of three weddings a day.

A. The common loon

41

And here we are at last, the Twin Cities of Minneapolis and St. Paul.

Awesome! Look, there are
skyscrapers and everything.

THE TWIN CITIES
OF MINNEAPOLIS
AND ST. PAUL

Yep. We're not in the prairie anymore. The tallest building is the IDS Tower, which stands 775 feet high. Almost half the people in Minnesota live in the Twin Cities area. Minneapolis is the bigger and busier of the two cities, and St. Paul is the state capital.

The cities are in part divided by the Mississippi River. Minneapolis grew up around St. Anthony Falls. It's the only major waterfall on the Mississippi River. Flour mills were built along the river, using the power of the waterfall. For a while the falls were the highest navigable point on the Mississippi and served as the endpoint for river traffic. By the 1870s, stone mills clustered around the falls to grind wheat from Minnesota farms.

Q. What poem did the United States' first famous poet Henry Wadsworth Longfellow write that was set at Minnehaha Falls?

Minneapolis produced more flour than any other city in the country for about 50 years.

The falls were reinforced with cement, and now they look more like a dam. But the riverfront has been restored into a really nice park and the historic Stone Arch Bridge has great views of the falls and the Mississippi. Nicollet Island below the falls is a fun place to visit and enjoy the river. Down river a few miles is the Minneheha Falls.

Minneapolis doesn't just boast falling waters—it also has "lakey" waters, too. In fact, it has 18 lakes, and the name "Minneapolis" actually means "city of water."

WIRthL.
CEDAR l.
LAKE of the ISLES
LAKE CALhoun
LAKE HARRiet
MINNEHAHA creek
MINNEAPOLIS
Downtown
LAKE NOKOMIS
LAKE HIAWatha

MINNEAPOLIS HAS 18 LAKES

More lakes?!

A. "The Song of Hiawatha," the romantic story of a Native American maiden.

THE SCULPTURE GARDEN IN MINNEAPOLIS HAS LOTS OF UNUSUAL ART

Minneapolis has a lot going for it. It's the financial and cultural center of the northern Great Plains. Its museums are among the finest in the nation. The Walker Art Center has a famous collection of contemporary art, and it shares its building with the Guthrie Center, a renowned theater. Across the way is the Sculpture Garden, seven acres covered in funky outdoor sculptures—there's even one of a giant spoon holding an enormous cherry. The Minneapolis Institute of Art has everything from works by Pablo Picasso to an incredible collection of art from the American West. Some people say that Minneapolis has more theaters per person than any city in the United States except New York.

Minneapolis is also home to three major sports teams. The Hubert H. Humphrey Metrodome Stadium hosts the Minnesota Twins baseball team and the Minnesota Vikings football team. The Minnesota Timberwolves basketball team plays at the Target Center at the Metrodome. And the University of Minnesota, which is right on the river, sponsors 11 sports (both men's and women's) that compete at the NCAA (National Collegiate Athletic

Q. Where can you find a skeleton of the diplodocus, one of the longest dinosaurs?

44

Association) Division I level. The university is one of the largest in the country, and has about 50,000 students.

Remember I mentioned that Minneapolis has skyways that were built so people can get around without going out into the cold? Well, you can see them everywhere in the city. They help make Minneapolis both a warmer place to live and a more interesting place to look at.

THE METRODOME STADIUM HOSTS THE MINNESOTA TWINS BASEBALL TEAM AND THE MINNESOTA VIKINGS FOOTBALL TEAM

What about St. Paul?

St. Paul is 10 miles to the east. It's a quieter city with more neighborhoods and fewer big buildings. Let's head over and take a look.

A. At the Science Museum of Minnesota in St. Paul, where there is an 82-foot-long skeleton. The diplodocus was a kind of sauropod, a family of large, long-necked plant-eaters.

BONJOUR!

PIG's

ST. PAUL WAS ORIGINALLY
CALLED PIG'S EYE

St. Paul looks like a pretty nice place to live.

It is, but it didn't start out that way. St. Paul was originally named Pig's Eye, after a French trapper who built a tavern here. A lot of troublemakers hung out here until missionaries came to convert the townspeople and rename the town. St. Paul grew faster than Minneapolis at first, so when Minnesota became a state, it became the state capital. The capitol building is a beautiful domed marble structure. It's really spectacular inside, kind of like the inside of one of those huge European cathedrals. There's a terrific children's museum with all sorts of fun activities. And, finally, there's the Fitzgerald Theater, where the famous writer and radio man Garrison Keillor hosts his show, "A Prairie

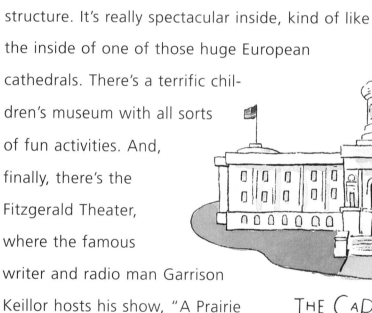

THE CAPITOL BUILDING

Q. What was the tallest ice structure ever built?

Home Companion." On the show he tells stories about Lake Wobegon, an imaginary town that's very similar to the places we've visited on our trip through Minnesota.

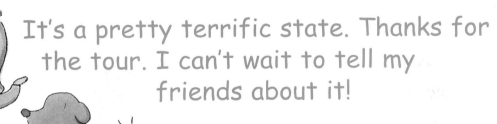

GARRISON KEILLOR HOSTS "A PRAIRIE HOME COMPANION"

Well, that was great! Minnesota's a pretty cool place—and I don't just mean it's neat, it's nice and cold, too.

Yep, it is pretty cool. One hundred and fifty years ago Minnesota was a lot of prairie and forests and icy trading posts. Today, it's one of the handsomest, pleasantest states in the nation.

It's a pretty terrific state. Thanks for the tour. I can't wait to tell my friends about it!

I CAME OUT TO WARM UP!

 A tremendous ice palace built in the 1992 St. Paul Winter Carnival was taller than 150 feet and made out of 25,000 blocks of i

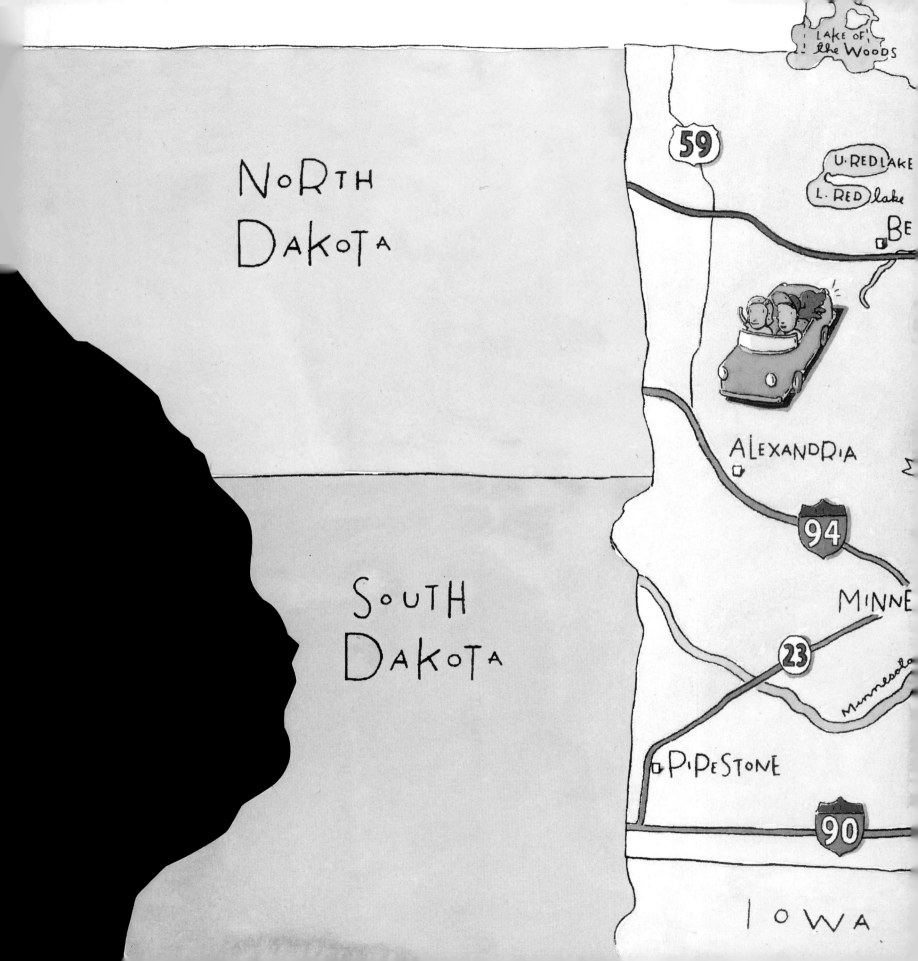

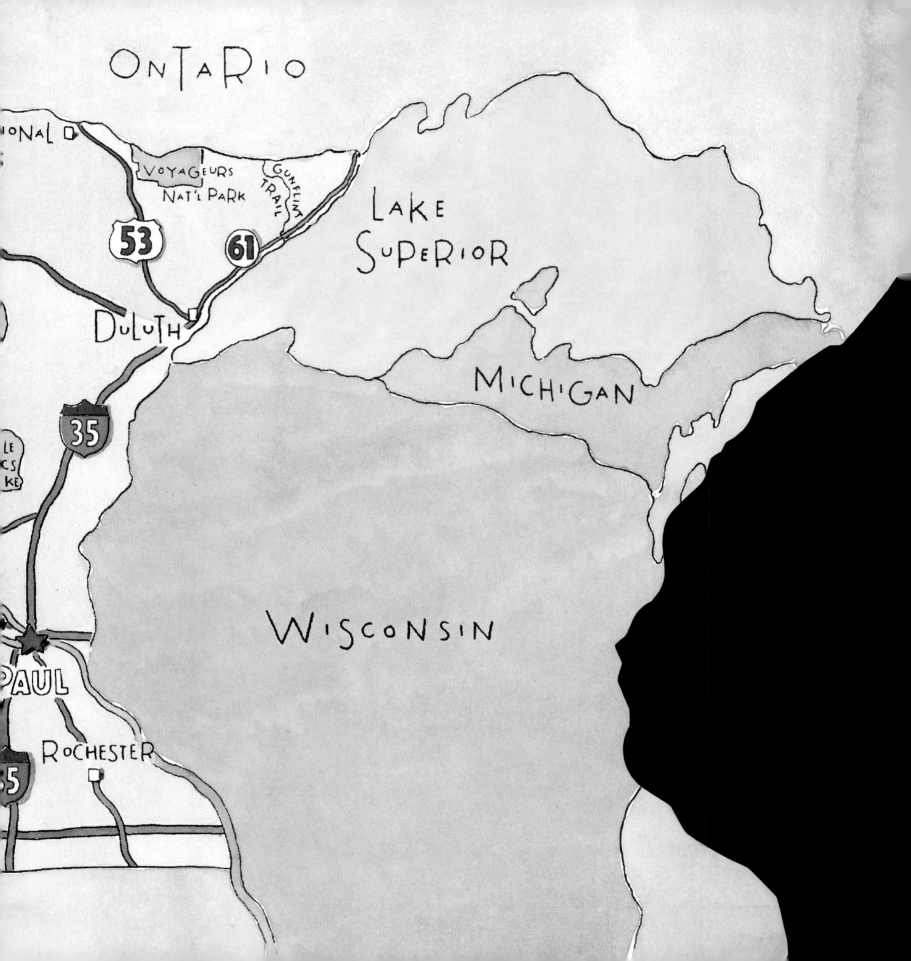